About the author

Jane Adshead-Grant has over 25 years' experience working within global financial and professional services as both an HR practitioner and an accredited coach with the International Coach Federation and Time to Think. Jane is also a member of the Association for Coaching and the NeuroLeadership Institute.

Jane is passionate about listening to others and creating the opportunity for them to think well for themselves in order to facilitate their personal growth. Jane has developed her own listening skills through her personal leadership development and coach training and in particular through her work with Nancy Kline, the pioneer of the Thinking Environment®. The Thinking Environment is a way of being which seeks to generate high-quality independent thinking. It comprises ten components representing the way we behave around each other. You can learn more about the Thinking Environment and its applications by visiting the website www.timetothink.com.

Developing the art of active listening can be a game changer as you develop your leadership skills. Your ability to listen well to others will reap huge benefits, personally and professionally. You will develop your own thinking, creativity and confidence, and could even find yourself promoted as your ability to get the most out of your team is recognised and valued.

Jane is also wife to Ed and mum to two daughters. When she's not listening to others, she spends her time walking their dog Charlie and learning Spanish.

To contact and keep up-to-date with Jane go to: www.janeadsheadgrant.com

Acknowledgements

In writing this book I would like to acknowledge all those who have helped me develop my listening skills – a passion of mine. I am grateful for being the coach I am and having the capacity to listen well for the benefit of my clients.

I am grateful to my family and friends who provide opportunities for me to listen more every day.

In particular, I would like to acknowledge Nancy Kline for teaching me the depth of listening and paying attention that ignites the minds of others.

I would like to thank Laura Wilson for helping me develop my online platform and who encouraged me to write this book.

This book was inspired by some wonderful people including: Kathryn, Natasha, Ben, Adrian, Karla, Andrew, Allan, Rina, and many more who I've had the privilege of working with and listening to in order to generate more of their independent thinking.

I am deeply grateful for my wonderful friends who have spent hours listening to me in return, and in particular, Elizabeth, Marion, Joanna, Georgina and Anne.

I would also like to thank Jo Johnston who spent many hours editing and proofreading my text which I am so grateful for. My mum and dad, my husband and our two girls who support me in all that I do – thank you for your encouragement and love.

Foreword

Are you listening or just waiting to speak? says without flinching what all of us want the bad listeners in our life to hear. And for many of us, that is just about everyone in our life! But this book does more than that. It helps us see that maybe the worst listener in our life is us. Remarkably, Jane makes it possible, even a bit fun, to face and change our own habits of interruption, of getting ready to reply, of valuing our own thoughts more than the forming thoughts of the other person. Most important, Jane makes it impossible any more to deny the fact that if we are leaders or professionals, the most important facet of our work has to be our listening.

The most. Everything follows from the quality of our listening. Her arguments, her references, and her 11 principles, 10 challenges and 5 tips make the whole challenge doable, starting today. Also, I

find it easy to absorb Jane's message because
she herself lives it.

**Nancy Kline, Pioneer of the Thinking
Environment®**
Author of Time to Think - Listening to Ignite the
Human Mind,
More Time to Think – a Way of Being in the World
Living with Time to Think – The Goddaughter
Letters.

Contents   **Page**

About this book

'When people are speaking, they require our undivided attention... It's called respect, it's called appreciation - and it's called leadership.' Frances Hesselbein, President and CEO of the Frances Hesselbein Leadership Institute[1]

Within our education system, our efforts from an early age are focused on reading, writing and speaking, all of which are essential communication skills. However, we are seldom taught the skill of listening. The essential skill of our capacity to listen well, to understand and to be understood is overlooked. When I say listening, I mean really listening, not just hearing the words and looking like we are giving attention, but listening until we gain new knowledge or

---

[1] Web: http://www.HesselbeinInstitute.org
Facebook: frances.hesselbein

insight from what is being said. Listening until we change.

Through reading this book, you will discover:

- Why listening is critical in life and business and could change your career
- The top five myths about listening – it's about what you can do not what you can't
- The 11 principles of active listening to help you get started
- The common challenges to active listening
- The benefits of active listening
- Ouch! Listening to feedback, how it's hard but necessary to hear what others think about you
- And finally, going undercover, with five easy-to-use tips to help you become a better listener.

Chapter 1

Why listening is critical in life and business

'Most people do not listen with intent to understand. They listen with the intent to reply.' – Stephen R. Covey

The importance of listening is that not only does it improve the quality of your leadership, but you will also gain commitment from others. Your team will learn to trust you and vice versa. By listening to others, you transmit great respect for them. If you go out and listen to your team, you will engage them in a very different way from if you go out to give orders. By listening to your team members' ideas, thoughts and possible solutions, building on them and following up on their contributions, you will see a higher level of motivation and commitment and their performance will improve dramatically. You will spend less time having to fix things as your team will be empowered to fix things themselves – they will be using their innovation and creativity to solve problems and drive the business forward – and all this as a result of your decision to simply listen.

Being able to listen well can lead to improved relationships both personally and professionally. It provides for greater clarity and fewer misunderstandings. Listening reveals more creative and innovative work. When we listen well to one another, without interruption, the brain relaxes and begins to form new connections. These new connections present creative and innovative ideas. Also when we listen to others, we develop our own ideas and innovations yet further. Many successful leaders will attribute their success to effective listening. Brian Tracy said[2]:

'Perhaps the most powerful of all leadership techniques for motivating employees is effective listening. Learning to practice your listening skills until it becomes a habit can do more to improve your relationships at work and at home than perhaps any other single behaviour.'

Great leaders are proactive, strategic and intuitive listeners. They enjoy listening rather than seeing it as a chore that they have to do. They recognise that knowledge and wisdom are not gained by talking, but by listening.

Reading this book has already shown you to be a great leader because it says that you want to learn more about the importance of listening and how you can develop your own skills further.

---

[2] http://www.briantracy.com/blog/leadership-success/motivating-employees-by-using-effective-listening-skills

Smart leaders know that there is far more to be gained by giving up the floor than by dominating it. One of the great challenges today is the speed at which we operate. Everyone seems to be in a rush to communicate what is on their mind, so much so that they miss out on the value of everything that can be gleaned from the thoughts of others. To be a greater leader, you need to be a great communicator and to be a great communicator you need to be a great listener.

Good listening skills also benefit us in our private life – having a deeper personal network, improving our confidence and self-esteem. We achieve more – in our studies with higher grades and in our work with better results. Good listening also improves our health and general wellbeing. Research has shown that speaking raises our blood pressure (as you may have experienced for yourself), but listening brings it down. Being a good listener requires heart and empathy. It requires a genuine desire to connect with the person as one human being to another. It is about building a relationship and there is no more powerful way to do this than with a genuine desire and effort to truly listen, to intuitively understand where others are coming from and what they are leaving unsaid. When this happens, it creates a strong bond that develops trust and respect for one another. We all value some friends over others due to how they interact with us and demonstrate how they value us.

Listening is not the same as hearing. Hearing refers to the sounds you perceive within earshot. It could be the gentle ticking of a clock in the background or it could be the noise of others in the room. Listening is an active pursuit. It requires focus and effort. Listening is about paying attention to what is being said, how it is being said and what is not being said, through non-verbal body language.

We spend a lot of time listening. Research suggests adults spend an average of 70 per cent of their time engaged in some sort of communication. Of this, an average of 45 per cent is spent listening compared to 30 per cent speaking, 16 per cent reading and 9 per cent writing[3].

> **Of the 45 per cent of our time spent listening, a person recalls 50 per cent of what they have just heard and only 20 per cent is remembered long-term.**

Listening is the psychological process of receiving, attending to, understanding and responding to the spoken or non-verbal

---

[3] Based on the research of: Adler, R., Rosenfeld, L. and Proctor, R. *Interplay: the process of interpersonal communicating,* Fort Worth, TX: Harcourt. (2001)

messages we receive. Hearing on the other hand is a physiological process – 85 per cent of what we know is from listening.

Listening is critical to both our personal and business life because it:

1. Helps others think well for themselves – when you pay attention to another and listen with curiosity to what they will say next, that person will be empowered and begin to think better as a result
2. Allows for clarity, creativity and confidence to emerge
3. Makes others feel valued and respected
4. Facilitates a more solution focused rather than problem-focused approach. Listening and waiting to see someone's potential will help them generate a solution rather than dwelling on the problem

5. Promotes greater accountability in others. When you listen to another by letting them know that their thinking matters, they will feel empowered, take on more responsibility and develop more self-belief

6. Unlocks the potential in others when you silently ask the question, 'Where might you go next with your thinking?' 'What more can you achieve?'

7. Listening is the most powerful form of acknowledgement; it is a way of saying you matter.

Nancy Kline, pioneer of the Thinking Environment has developed two types of listening – a listening to reply and a listening to ignite[4]. Listening to reply is where we listen just long enough to take in what the other person is saying in order to form a response, make a diagnosis, a judgement or

---

[4] N. Kline, *More Time to Think*. Octopus Publishing Group, London. UK (2009, 2015).

consider a solution. Essentially we wait until the other person has finished, or we may even interrupt and offer our reply. In contrast listening to ignite is where we offer our attention, keeping our eyes on the eyes of the speaker (not a glare, rather a soft gaze) and encouraging the speaker to continue. When listening to ignite, we listen without interrupting. We offer a sense of ease, free from rush and we offer an equality, which suggests that we both have the capacity to think well, even though our thoughts may be different. In my experience, it is when we listen to ignite the mind of another, that we provide one of the greatest gifts we, as human beings can offer one another.

As a leader you may assume that you need to have all the answers or at least the majority. After all your team looks to you to provide them with direction and create a culture for them to perform well and achieve success. Believing we have to have the answers can be dangerous because it limits a generation of independent thinking – for others to think well for themselves. When you consider your capacity to listen as one of your most valuable skills, you will naturally be in a state of curiosity – curious about your team member's or client's thoughts. When you are curious, you develop further your ability to ask great questions – questions that will help others to form their ideas, gain clarity, understand what is getting in the way of what they want and achieve breakthroughs.

Listening is an active skill.
Some people mistakenly assume listening is an opportunity to sit back and do nothing. On the contrary, listening requires skill, patience and self-discipline. For some of us, the desire to interrupt another person when they are speaking is just too strong. We congratulate ourselves on the fact that we can finish their sentence, usually someone we

know well. While this may feel like we have a deep connection with that person, we have, in fact, just hijacked their thinking and we are no longer listening.

When we are truly listening and our attention is solely given to another and they know they will not be interrupted, paradoxically their thinking improves. Research from MRI scans show that new neural pathways begin to form and new connections spring into action creating

Listening requires the self-discipline of allowing the other person to speak, free from interruption.

new ideas. Sometimes we are moved profoundly by what the other person says and we want to acknowledge them, comfort them or reassure them – all of which are natural responses. Similarly we may feel emotional, tearful or angry about has been said and feel obliged to respond.

When we actively listen to another, allowing them to continue with their thinking, we need the self-discipline to take note of our response to what has been said while simultaneously refocusing our attention back onto the speaker. This enables the speaker to continue their thinking well as they articulate their thoughts, rather than being interrupted or hijacked by our own emotional response.

Chapter 2

The top five myths about listening

Most people think that they are good listeners. However listening is a skill that we can all improve upon. Recognising the characteristics of poor listening can help us overcome our limitations and create new habits to listen actively. There are some common myths about listening that can influence the way we feel and make the listening process less effective, so it is helpful to be aware of these.

> Listening is an active process that we have to do consciously and we can get better, with practice.

1. It is difficult to learn how to listen

It is true that our world is increasingly noisier. We
are bombarded with communications and
distractions, making listening more difficult. In
fact, it's difficult today to escape sound
completely. In its 1999 *Guidelines for Community
Noise*, the World Health Organisation declared:
'Worldwide, noise-induced hearing impairment is
the most prevalent irreversible occupational
hazard and it is estimated that 120 million people
worldwide have disabling hearing difficulties.'[5]
However, our ability to listen well depends upon
the circumstances of the communication, our
personality and whether we want to listen or not!

---

[5] http://www.ncbi.nlm.nih.gov/pmc/articles/PMC1253729/

> **The ability to actively listen well to another is one of the greatest gifts we have as a human being. So it is worth putting in the effort to practise developing the fundamental skills of listening.**

The skills for active listening are not difficult, but do require practice. As a leader, you will be acknowledged for your ability to listen well, you will get results and others will want to follow you. You will also discover benefits in your social life – you will enjoy stronger relationships and gain a deeper understanding of others.

2. Intelligent people are better at listening

There is no link between our cognitive intelligence and how well we listen. We might assume because someone is bright and articulates well, that they are naturally better listeners. While they may be able to consume and process more information quickly, they are not necessarily better listeners. For example, a very bright person may tune out of a conversation, as they believe they have heard all they need to hear, rather than waiting and listening for the potential in another.

People with a higher emotional intelligence (EQ) are more likely to be better listeners. Our EQ refers to our ability to understand and accept ourselves, seek to understand others, and manage our emotions in order to deal with the daily challenges of life. A key dimension of EQ is empathy – our ability to step into the shoes of another. When we are able to quieten our own emotional reaction and give our attention to another person, we are able to truly listen.

We all have preferences in the way we absorb information. Through my studies in neuro-linguistic programming, I was introduced to the concept of representational systems. There are four main systems:

- Visual: the process of translating communication into pictures
- Auditory: the process of translating communication into sounds
- Kinaesthetic: the process of checking communication with our feelings
- Audio digital: the process of internally checking communication by talking to ourselves.

Being familiar with your own preference is useful in knowing where you can focus your attention in developing your listening skills. For example, someone who may have a preference for translating information into pictures may find themselves wandering off drawing images in their mind as they listen. Someone who has a kinaesthetic preference may check their own feelings as they are listening. There is no right or wrong way to process the information, it is just that we all have different preferences and you may have more than one. For example, I have a dual preference of auditory and kinaesthetic.

3. Hearing and listening are the same

The fact that you might have good hearing does not mean that you are necessarily a good listener. Hearing is sensory and involuntary – you will hear the sound of a clock ticking or the hum of a machine in the background. However listening requires your commitment and perception.

As an effective listener, you will pick up on the non-verbal signals of the speaker such as their tone, gestures, pace and volume. Active listening requires you to use all of your senses in order to understand the meaning of what is being said.

4. Listening comes from maturity

People do not necessarily become better listeners as they get older or if they have more responsibility. They may become wiser due to their life experiences; however they are not automatically better listeners. Without practice and the conscious effort to practice effective listening, there is no guarantee listening will get better – in fact it may actually get worse.

It is easy to pick up bad habits for listening just as it is for other skills that we often use. As confidence improves, we tend to pick up bad habits – rather like driving a car. When we first set out, having just passed our driving test, we follow the guidelines of mirror, signal, and manoeuvre. However as we become more confident, we are more likely to become lazy and fall into autopilot mode. Some of the bad habits that we can potentially fall into when thinking we are listening include:

- Interrupting and jumping to conclusions
- Waiting to speak and hurrying the person
- Making assumptions based on our preconceptions
- Repeatedly re-emphasising our own view.

5. Gender affects our ability to listen well

It is true to say that men and women communicate differently. Women tend to place a higher value on connection, cooperation and emotional messages and men are more action orientated, concerned with facts and may feel uncomfortable talking about emotions.

This does not mean that women are better listeners than men or vice versa. Men and women are likely to ask different types of questions of the speaker in order to clarify or understand the message; therefore their final interpretation of the message may be different.

Chapter 3

The 11 principles of active listening

During my work as a coach, I have listened to clients on occasion for just for 45 minutes and within that time they achieve a transformation in the way they think about their issue and create a new strategy for moving forward. An experience I had with a client still stays in my mind, based on his creativity and all that he achieved for himself in just 45 minutes. James came to me and asked for some coaching to develop his business. He is successful in his field and yet over the past year had witnessed a drop in winning new business. One of James's strengths is that he is very adaptable and offers his clients a flexible approach that best suits them. As he began to describe his situation, he discovered that he was in fact unclear about his own offering. He was not sure how to present himself in order to compel his client to select him.

James came up with a stunning metaphor when describing himself and his offering – like a white-water raft. He would be in the raft with his clients and navigate the river with them, pausing before the rapids to jointly decide which was the best side of the river to follow, and then accompanying them through the rapids, continually adjusting to the speed and direction of the water and encouraging his clients to respond with agility to what they were facing.

Following this creative thinking, James became clear about what he offered his clients and how he would communicate this succinctly in the future. Additionally, James became visibly more confident through our interaction and realised he had made progress.

Today, James continues to develop his business and win new clients on a regular basis, sustaining the income he had set for himself.

My part in this exchange was a paradox – whilst I was essential in my ability to listen well, ask questions and not interrupt, I was in fact irrelevant. It was James who created his new winning strategy and the results spoke for themselves.

Over the years, I have discovered **11 principles** that can really make a difference in how you develop your active listening skills:

Number 1:
Don't interrupt

When we interrupt someone, it is as if we have just hijacked their thinking. We have completely stopped their train of thought. You may want to interrupt just as they take breath to continue. Stop yourself and allow the person to complete their thinking.

Notice the internal noise in your own mind. Notice any feelings that have emerged as a result of what you have just heard – accept them

Number 2:

Quieten your own mind

and refocus your attention on the speaker. Clear your own mind of any distracting thoughts, such as wondering what you'll make for dinner that night!

Number 3:

Be at ease, free from urgency

Relax, smile and let the speaker know that you are interested in what they have to say. Notice your own body language; let it communicate that the speaker matters. Be open and engaging. Keep your eyes on the eyes of the speaker, a soft gaze. Keep nodding to a minimum so it does not confuse the speaker and convey the message that you want them to hurry up.

Give your full attention to the speaker. Close down the laptop; turn your mobile phone on silent. Ensure that you don't need a comfort

Number 4:

Eliminate distractions

break or your stomach is rumbling or that you are so tired you cannot focus. Ensure your personal needs have been attended to.

Number 5:

Be open-minded

Put yourself in the shoes of the other person. Be empathetic and look at the issues from their perspective.

You may not agree with what you have just heard, but before you jump to a conclusion, listen more, and then listen once more.

People often feel obliged to make a noise or interrupt in some way after just six seconds due to feeling uncomfortable with silence. You may have heard the phrase, let silence do the

Number 6:

Use silence

heavy lifting. When you are silent, the speaker has the capacity to work through many challenges. It takes time for others to formulate their thoughts – give them the time to do so.

Number 7:

Be objective

Be aware of your own personal prejudice. Don't allow the style or habits of the speaker to distract you from what they are communicating. Acknowledge the diversity of thinking and speaking. If you cannot hear them clearly, ask them to speak slowly or louder. Be accommodating to those who may feel shy or nervous.

Pay attention to what is not being said. Notice the speed, tone and volume of the speaker when they are communicating their message – what are they emphasising or rushing over? Are they averting your eyes

Number 8:

Notice non-verbal body language

continually to avoid seeing your response? Are they saying something verbally and yet their body is saying something different with their gestures?

Number 9:

Listen for potential

Listen for where the speaker is going with their thinking. One of the most profound skills of listening is generating the thinking in others – enabling them to make new connections and to reveal new insights. You can master this with practice, by applying these 11 principles.

The mind works best in the presence of a question. Laura Berman Fortgang developed Wisdom Accessing Questions (WAQ) [6].The

Number 10:

Ask questions

common thread to these questions is that they all begin with what. For example, 'What do you want to achieve?' 'What is stopping you from taking the next step?' 'What do you need now to move forward?'

---

[6] L. Berman Fortgang, *Living your best life.* Penguin Putnam Inc, New York. (2001).

Number 11:

Leave your ego at the door

Listening is an active skill that requires effort. It also requires effort to leave your ego at the door in order to provide a quality of listening that will enable others to shine. Spare the advice. This well-meaning behaviour disrupts the listening process and forces the person to listen to what we have to say. You never know what you might miss when you fill the space with your words.

It requires a conscious decision on your part to listen and seek to understand what the speaker is saying. Stephen Covey, author of The Seven Habits of Highly Effective People, suggests that the key to being highly successful is: 'Seek to understand before being understood.'

> **Active listening is a skill and it is something that you can develop further. Just like going to the gym and developing your muscle and stamina, you can develop your listening skills with regular and disciplined practice.**

Active listening also requires patience, being free from urgency. If you truly do not have time to engage in a meaningful conversation with someone who has requested to speak with you – let them know that while you don't have sufficient time now, you can find a mutually convenient time in the future when you can make the time, after all you want to provide an opportunity for the person to explore their thoughts and feelings, create new ideas, reveal potential opportunities and enjoy the results.

Test your own active listening skills

To test your own active listening skills, have a go at this online two-minute listening practice test[7] to determine how well you are listening.
You may be surprised by the results – I was! The key is not to make assumptions or fill in the gaps with your own interpretation.

Alternatively complete this multiple choice test[8] to discover where you can focus your own development for listening more actively.

---

[7] www.wisc-online.com/learn/listening-practice
[8] http://psychologytoday.tests.

Chapter 4

The common challenges to active listening

'I like to listen, I have learned a great deal from listening carefully. Most people never listen.' – Ernest Hemmingway

Some people have mastered the art of pretending to listen or even selective listening. This happens for me at home sometimes when I provide some information to my husband about something we are doing later in the day and may tell him two or three times. When it comes to the time to go or do what we have arranged, he has forgotten all about it. Clearly, he was not really listening when I was speaking!

Some of the common challenges to active listening include:

1. Being driven by the need to interrupt. We find ourselves desperately wanting to offer a response, give a direction or correct what has just been said.

   Research has shown that for every 300 thoughts a person has, only 30 are expressed. This suggests that there will be so much more going on for the speaker than we will ever be able to determine. This statistic helped me to appreciate that it is only when the speaker has finished that I will either ask another question or provide the information that they may have requested.

2. The desire to have our own voice heard. In our more open-plan office environments, those who contribute quickly or more loudly are often applauded, rather than those who require more time to offer their response. Some

people feel that they need to speak to feel like they have made a contribution. This is important, especially when we are asked for our thoughts or opinions, but when we are truly listening to another, it is our respect for the other that we offer when we stay silent, until they have finished speaking.

3. Thinking what we are about to say is of more value than what the speaker is about to say. While this may be the case in some situations, we do not know that for sure. So listening with our attention, eyes focused on their eyes, wondering where they go may go next, will help the speaker in their thought processes as they articulate what it is they want to say.

4. Distractions are a constant challenge to our listening – from busy, noisy environments to mobile phones ringing or buzzing or the sound of an email arriving. To listen well to another,

we need to remove those distractions or quieten them as much as we can.

5. Allowing our own response to what the person is saying take over and distract us, therefore limiting our capacity to listen. We may become self-absorbed by the impact of what the person has just said and are more focused on ourselves rather than the person speaking.

6. Our own upbringing and school environments inadvertently promote boldness and more extroverted types, encouraging others to speak up now rather than reflect and take time. The way we learn to listen from a young age is by modelling it from those around us – our parents, our siblings, our teachers. In some families, if you don't speak up, you may be

To listen IS to contribute.

46

overlooked. You may have been positively encouraged to contribute to the family discussions on a regular basis. On the other hand, you may have been asked to listen quietly before speaking or you may have been used to a dialogue where others continually interrupt each other and there is little evidence of anyone listening. You may have heard many misunderstandings – often as a result of poor listening. As we mature and recognise the importance of listening and the impact it has for us, we can make the choice for ourselves.

7. Personality types can have an impact on our listening. Those with a more extroverted personality, based on the Myers Briggs Type Indicator, are more likely to speak up, feel more comfortable introducing themselves to those they don't know well and take more airtime in conversation than those with an

introverted personality. This is because the more extroverted personality receives their energy from external sources – from other people. Just because you may be an extrovert, doesn't mean you are not a good listener. The key is to be aware of your own preferences, and learn to listen well, not interrupt, and ensure you are not taking a disproportionate amount of time in conversations.

8. Our own body language can be a challenge to listening. Nodding our head gently can be seen as an affirmative action. It can be considered as an encouragement. While your intention may be positive, sometimes excessively nodding may affirm an unhelpful assumption the speaker has just declared. Similarly, rapid nodding may communicate that the speaker should speed up. It may signal, 'I get the gist of what you are saying

and what I need to hear.' Other signals that can be a barrier to listening is when we avert our eye contact – we look out the window, at the computer screen or the television! Our posture can signal whether we are ready to listen or not. Sitting back on our chair, arms folded and legs crossed is not a particularly inviting pose that says you're ready to listen.

9. Being preoccupied when we have a lot on our mind can prevent us from truly listening. If we are stressed or under time pressure ourselves, this will limit our ability to listen well.

10. Note taking is a challenge to effective listening. As soon as we remove our eye contact from the speaker, we have lost the connection, our attention and we can no longer be truly listening. Instead we are considering what to write, how to summarise what we have just heard into a note. Coaches

often ask me if they can take notes during a coaching session with their clients. Managers ask me the same, during conversations they have with their team members.

In my experience, taking notes acts a distraction for you and the other person. They may be worried about what you are writing (even if they can read upside down). You cannot listen and write at the same time – listening is one thing that our brain cannot multitask. Earl Miller, a neuroscientist at the Massachusetts Institute of Technology and one of the world experts on divided attention, says that our brains are 'not wired to multitask well. When people think they're multitasking, they're actually just switching from one task to another very rapidly. And every time they do, there's a cognitive cost in doing so.' You will have experienced this I am sure when you are speaking and the other person says I'm listening, but then promptly turns to her laptop and responds to an email. I recommend taking 10 minutes after a meeting to capture the essential notes. If you have listened well, you will recall the key points from any meeting or conversation.

Be aware of your own weaknesses in listening. Perhaps you are impatient or perhaps you are notorious for interrupting. Tom Peters suggests that most managers are 18-second listeners! That is how long they can listen for before they interrupt. Do these habits describe you? Be honest with yourself and seek feedback from others as to how well they think you listen In his book, Power Listening: Mastering the Most Critical Business Skill of All, Bernard T. Ferrari, identifies six types of poor listeners[9]:

---

[9] B.T Ferrarri, *Power Listening: Mastering the Most Critical Business Skill of All.* Penguin Group, New York (2012).

- The Opinionator – squelches ideas that don't match their own and listens only to reload their own defence
- The Grouch – everyone else's ideas are simply wrong
- The Preambler – takes the long route in, self-serving and questions are to conceal their own poor listening
- The Perseverator – talks a lot but doesn't say much and does not advance the conversation
- The Answer Man/Woman – spouts out a solution before all the information is laid out or there is a consensus of what the challenge might actually be and is desperate to impress
- The Pretender – not really interested in what you are saying; feigns engagement and may already have made up their mind.

So how can you tell when someone is not really listening and they are adopting one of these roles?

- Lack of eye contact with you. This can sometimes reflect a sign of shyness or a degree of discomfort in the listener.
- A disengaged posture. Someone who is slouched, leaning back or even swinging on their chair suggests they're not listening well.
- Being distracted. Someone who is constantly fidgeting or yawning!
- Inappropriate gestures or expressions. Someone who looks disinterested gazes out of the window or at their watch.
- Introducing a sudden change of topic. When the listener changes the nature of the conversation as if to say that they've heard enough and want to move on.
- Daydreaming. This can occur when a listener hears something that sets off a chain of

thoughts or ideas in their head and they go off into their own world and have a slightly glazed look.

Chapter 5

The benefits of active listening

Recognising the benefits of listening to others is a powerful way to change any bad habits. It gives us a purpose to change.

When you listen actively, you will:

- Learn more for yourself – gain new knowledge, enhance your understanding and even develop a new skill.

- Help others think well for themselves. By offering your undivided attention to another that is free from urgency, the other person will develop their thinking and be able to articulate their message more clearly.

- Create new opportunities for yourself and others. Listening is a catalyst for creation and change.

- Develop new insights. New insights emerge when you are relaxed, free from competition and stress. You may have experienced that a new insight suddenly strikes you about what you have just been working on when you take a break or do something unrelated to work – such as going for a run. In this situation, you have been tapping into your inner wisdom, listening to what is within you.

- Enhance your relationships. Listening is one of the most valuable gifts we can give another human being. It makes others feel valued and empowered; that they are worth your time and that you are interested in them.

- Take your communication skills to a higher level. Listening is an essential skill both in our personal lives and our business. Richard Branson, in an interview with Entrepreneur magazine said[10]: '*If you want to stand out as a leader, a good place to begin is by listening. Any organisation's best assets are its people, and if you are ready to help the team to achieve its goals, you can start gathering information on how to move things along just by paying attention to what employees are saying.*'

> **Listening can solve or even prevent conflict, it reduces misunderstanding and it generates possibilities, opportunities and results.**

---

[10] http://www.entrepreneur.com/article/231826

- Developing your capacity to listen actively will also develop your skill of asking great questions. We have already discovered the WAQ questions from Laura Berman Fortgang[11]. I remember a former boss always being quiet in our monthly HR meetings. He looked pensive throughout and waited for others to share their views and ideas. And then he would ask a question, a simple question, for example, 'What if we were to focus on the best outcome from this situation, what would we do?' It was often this question that would transform the outcome of the meeting. What stood out for me was his ability to listen, to be free of judgement and allow his team to formulate their ideas. He provided us with space, an appreciation of our diversity of thinking and an equality that suggested our thoughts were as meaningful as his own.

---

[11] L Berman Fortgang, *Living your best life*. Penguin Putnam Inc, New York (2001).

Asking great questions will come as a result of your capacity to listen well. One question alone can change the course of success.

Chapter 6

Ouch! Listening to feedback

'It is through listening you will cultivate wisdom and be able to remove ignorance.' - Dalai Lama

Not all listening is an enriching experience. Listening to negative feedback is not always easy; sometimes it's unpleasant, awkward and downright difficult. Sometimes we are prepared for the conversation, other times we are not. Feedback can be delivered in different ways, some more effective than others. Good feedback will be based on evidence – what the person has seen, heard or felt in relation to you and your performance. It may also be based on what others have experienced of you.

I was at my local Speakers Club earlier this year and I noticed a new member. I introduced myself and asked about his interest in the club. He went on to tell me that he had been a member for over a year, however from a previous competition night he had received feedback on his two-minute topic speech that had set him back. So much so, he had not wanted to return to the club for a year! I was happy to acknowledge his courage in returning and for wanting to develop his public-speaking skills afresh. One of the benefits of our Speakers Club is that following your speech, you are given an evaluation immediately afterwards. This provides on the spot feedback in a safe and nurturing environment. Being an evaluator develops and takes our listening to a new level. While we intend our evaluations to reflect the values of the club, coming from a place of respect, integrity, service and excellence, we cannot know how the speaker will receive the feedback.

61

Listening to feedback is a time when you may want to clarify information and to clearly understand what is being said. You may need to paraphrase what you have just head, not only to check your understanding, but also that you have listened well. When listening to some of my clients, I can hear their frustration and disappointment in what they have heard from feedback.

The frustration often comes in the form of a request that they adopt a different style – a different personality style such as being more extroverted. On other occasions I hear frustration as a result of misunderstanding or a lack of clarity in expectations.

When we are listening to feedback and feel a reaction spark, we may begin to stop listening and formulate a response: 'That is not what happened', 'How dare you say that' or 'I don't believe it, it's not fair – I worked so hard on that project.' As soon as you notice this reaction, that is the moment to engage your self-discipline, dig deep and really, really listen. It may be that you need to ask a question to clarify, to support the evidence or to gain a different perspective on the situation.

A personal example of mine is when I received feedback on my coaching at the end of last year and I took it badly! I surprised myself as to how much it affected me. I realised that I was not perhaps in the best mood to receive the feedback. It came at the end of a very busy week and I was tired. I had been working really hard and specifically on this particular aspect of my coaching. I needed to record some of my coaching sessions for my next level of accreditation. It requires effort to arrange the recordings and permission from the client to use them. On this occasion, I thought it was a good recording that demonstrated the particular areas of my coaching that I was focusing on. The feedback was unexpected and a blow! I began to doubt myself.

After a few days and taking a step back from the feedback, as well as asking others, I realised that this was just one person's perspective. I also recognised that we had different styles and different backgrounds in our coaching approach. I have much admiration for the person who gave me the feedback and I was able to stand back and realise the gift she was giving me. While I had not realised this at the time, it has been very helpful to bring her perspective alongside my own to refine the aspect of coaching I wanted to work on.

When you have truly listened to the feedback and gained a new perspective, remember YOU have the choice. You can take the feedback on board or ignore it. I take feedback as a gift. If someone is prepared to offer me feedback, I know that I have the choice as to whether to act upon it or not. Being open-minded and willing to practice listening actively will provide you with greater choice.

Chapter 7

Going undercover – five tips to help you become a better listener

The television programme Undercover Boss is a great example of where the CEO of an organisation seeks to listen to their employees to find out what improvements can be made within the company. Each episode features a high-ranking executive or the owner of a corporation going undercover as a junior employee.

The CEO alters their appearance and assumes an alias and fictional backstory. The fictitious explanation given for the accompanying film crew is that the executive is being filmed as part of a documentary about junior workers in a particular industry. The CEO spends approximately one or two weeks undercover working in various areas of their company's operations, with a different job and in most cases a different location each day. They are exposed to a series of predicaments, often with amusing results, and they spend time getting to know the people who work in the company, learning about their professional and personal challenges. This experience often surprises the CEOs as they have little knowledge of what is going on at the grass roots level within their company.

At the end of their time undercover, the CEO returns to their true identity and asks the individual employees that they worked with to travel to a central location – often corporate headquarters. There they reveal their identity, and reward hard-working employees through promotion or financial benefits; while other employees are given training or better working conditions.

The programme demonstrates how important it is to listen to your employees, to understand what issues and challenges they face and to listen to their ideas for improvements.

The programme concludes with the CEO holding a companywide meeting where they share what they learned through going undercover. This has a knock-on effect across the company and others feel engaged and motivated by the fact the boss took the time and effort to listen. So how about you – would you consider going undercover?

If you answered yes and want to learn more from your employees by going undercover or even better, proactively going out and listening to them, here are **five tips** to help you become a better listener:

1. **Make time to listen** – we all have the same amount of time in our day – it is how we prioritise our time that makes the difference.

You can add real value to another person's
day, even their world, by listening to them.
Wisdom comes from all those around you, not
just your boss – it can come from anywhere
when you are prepared to listen. Expand your
own sphere of influence and gain different
perspectives from those with different
experiences and backgrounds.

2. **It's not about you** – don't worry about what
   you are going to say and pay attention to what
   is being said. Don't listen to have your ego
   stroked or your views agreed with, listen to be
   challenged and to learn something new. If you
   want to be listened to, be graceful and give
   others the gift of listening to them.

3. **Listen to the non-verbal messages** – people
   often communicate as much, if not more, with
   their body language, their actions and their
   facial expressions. Don't be fooled into

thinking that someone is not saying something just because they've not spoken. More often people will hold back from verbally communicating their disagreement or opposition, but they will almost certainly let you know that is how they are feeling with their non-verbal messages!

4. **Make listening part of your personal brand**
   – being recognised in this way will create opportunities for you and take you places that talking never could. Listening is a way that shows you respect and value others and it is the first and critical step in building trust.

> One of the greatest compliments you can have personally and professionally is to be known as a great listener.

5. **Appreciate the contribution of others** – one of the most overlooked aspects of listening is thanking others for their contributions. If you benefitted from listening to someone, let them know and thank them. Even if you do not recognise any specific value for you at that time, thank them for their time and input. Always remember to acknowledge those who contribute their energy, ideas or results.

'Active listening is a habit as well as the foundation of effective communication. Listening is one of the greatest gifts we can give another human being. You will motivate and engage others more effectively through your capacity to listen well. As a great listener, you are a great leader. As a great listener you can create a culture of courage, creativity and high performance. Apply the 11 principles of

active listening, catch yourself if you slip into any bad habits and you will stand out as an outstanding individual.'

April 2015

Reviews

"I think that this book is hugely important. It is wonderfully and uniquely focused, like a laser, on this central and crucial aspect of leadership and professional work. Best of all, your message is indelible because it is not diluted, and because you combine principles and ideas with the most practical, implementable actions. And so your book can truly change the way people behave and think. I am so glad you have produced this for the world!" **Nancy Kline, Author of More Time to Think – A way of being in the world.**

"Jane's easily digestible book is a clear and pragmatic guide and toolkit for leaders and managers at work and, well, just about anyone who wants to communicate and influence more effectively! It is full of intelligent perspectives on listening and its principles, challenges and benefits, highlighting the importance and impact

of good quality listening, recognising the challenges and pitfalls into which we can all too easily fall - and what to focus on to make a difference for others, and yourself. Jane brings great warmth and huge experience to the subject, bringing it alive with examples and connections to everyday life. Read this and you may enter a whole new world of rich information and understanding that you never knew existed while you were just waiting for the opportunity to say what you already knew." **Adrian Goodall, Executive Coach**

A quick and essential read for anyone who wants to improve their impact and relationships both in and out of work. Jane captures the contribution we can make as leaders by truly listening in every aspect of our lives. The tips help provide structure for practising these listening skills, which we often unconsciously neglect." **Kathryn Marriott, Head of Commerical Marketing, Global Group**

Notes

Notes

Notes

Notes

Made in the USA
Charleston, SC
06 July 2015